YOUR LIFE IS WHAT YOU MAKE IT

Strive to make it what YOU want it to be.

YOUR LIFE IS WHAT YOU MAKE IT

Strive to make it what YOU want it to be.

EVERLEAN MERRITT – (WILLIAMS)

Your Life Is What You Make It
Strive to make it what you want it to be.
Copyright © 2019 by Everlean Merritt – (Williams)

Library of Congress Control Number: 2019917755
ISBN-13:   Paperback: 978-1-950073-95-5
          ePub: 978-1-950073-96-2

Religion / Inspirational

All rights reserved. No part of this publication may be reproduced, distributed, or transmitted in any form or by any means, including photocopying, recording, or other electronic or mechanical methods, without the prior written permission of the publisher or author, except in the case of brief quotations embodied in critical reviews and certain other noncommercial uses permitted by copyright law.

Although every precaution has been taken to verify the accuracy of the information contained herein, the author and publisher assume no responsibility for any errors or omissions. No liability is assumed for damages that may result from the use of information contained within.

Printed in the United States of America

GoToPublish LLC
1-888-337-1724
www.gotopublish.com
info@gotopublish.com

Contents

Introduction 1

Standing at a Crossroad..4

Understanding the Threefold Purpose.............................10

God Is Amazing..22

A Celebration Time for Me 31

Book Celebration 34

Remarks from the Author 50

Encouragement for Growth 53

Words of Appreciation 55

Author's Profile..57

**Walk in the Light . . . God Is the Light!
Be Obedient and Let Him Lead You!**

Inside of you, there might be a weak heart.

But behind you is a

strong God!

Step *out* on *faith* and see what happens.

When you think

you are down to

nothing

know that

God is up to

something.

So don't stop

serving Him!

—based on Proverbs 16

To my wonderful husband,
SFC Theodore (Ted) Merritt.

To my joyful great-granddaughter,
Amiyah D. Caldwell

Ted is always there for me and inspires me to fulfill my dreams, use my talents, knowledge, and wisdom to encourage others to trust God and turn their visions to reality. I am blessed to have Ted in my life. He is a loving and caring person to anyone he meets. To me, he is a wonderful friend, sweetheart, husband, and the love of my life!

Amiyah displays a unique personality to ensure that she gets what she wants. She expresses that by standing alone and watching you. If she feels comfortable with you, she might come to you. At this early time of three years of age, I accept her ways. In the end, I will win. We love her dearly!

Introduction

Faith-Believing-Potential!

This story and message is written to encourage you. It will remind you that *all* things are possible when you trust and believe in God. It will help you to move forward, because you know that God will be with you. Show Him that you are His child and you are seeking Him for directions and guidance. Watch how He works through you, and you will see how blessed you are once you accept His invitation to serve Him and others. *He expects us to do that.* We are somebody... pick up your dream, and let God guide *you*! *Yes, He will do it!*

There is a *gift* in all of us! Will we explore it or just leave it?

There is a *story* in all of us; will we tell it or just keep it?

There is *potential* in all of us; will we use it or just let it die?

There is a *song* inside of us, will we sing it, or just keep it inside?

You have a God-given *life*; will you live it or just throw it away?

You have a heart of *love*; will you express it or just keep it?

How can you say no to God?

We were born to love, serve, and praise God!

On our journey, we have a purpose!

Learning to inspire and to be inspired should be rewarding to everyone! Also, listening, thinking, accepting, and believing are the keys to *achieving*.

Asking God for guidance and following His directions is your *foundation*.

And the ability to express your imagination is your *reward*.

Those will bring success, help you achieve a goal, and give you *victory*.

In one of Myles Munroe's books, he encouraged us to *tap the untapped and release the reservoir!*

Which means *releasing your potentials*.

Everyone is given gifts and talents. So we should use them by serving, giving, helping, and believing that we can do *anything* we set our minds to do, *with the help of the Lord*. Yes, we can do it, when we put our trust in Him.

There were times in my life when I thought about writing a book about my life. And when thoughts would come to me, I would think for a while and say, *No that is not something I wanted to do and if I did write it, what would I do with it?* Even though my mind was saying I don't want to write a story, I found myself keeping notes when things came to me and I never thought anything about it, other than keeping a record. But when I think about it now, *I was writing* . . . our minds are something else!

As a matter of fact, I have many pages that I have composed, but I never moved forward in trying to write a story. I went back occasionally and read the information that I had recorded; then I would put it back in the little black bag. I supposed I thought the materials were just for me, since I never did anything with them. It was never my plan to write a story about anyone. It was not something I thought I would do. I am still bewildered and can't believe that I did it. I believe that I was born for a purpose.

But I must say I am glad I was blessed and inspired by a vision to write a story that is now a book. And I am truly proud of it.

I am pleased to say that the writing of a story, the producing of a book, and the publishing of the life and legacy of a great servant are very rewarding to me. I thank God for choosing me to fulfill that *special* assignment.

Standing at a Crossroad

Sometimes, when you don't really know what to do or how to move forward, you will find yourself at a crossroad, thinking, *what shall I do?* You want to make the right decision that will help you, and at that point, you need to *envision* what it will take to start and finish an assignment. That is the question you must think about. It is important that you think about what you have to do once the book is written, so you will be prepared to move forward. I was not really prepared. One day a friend asked me, what are your plans for the book? I just looked and did not say anything. Later it came to me that finishing the book, was just the Beginning. I was caught in the Middle, later there would be an Ending and what am I going to do about the Sale of the book.

The beginning, the middle, the ending, and the sale!

Why?

You must first write a story to produce a book (the beginning). You must strive for a clear purpose for the reader (the middle). You must perform hard work to achieve your goal (the ending). You must have a unique cover that inspires the reader to buy (the sale).

The Beginning of the Experience

When I stopped and thought about everything, it came to me that we all have a purpose on earth. We may not know what our purpose is and maybe we don't understand. But if we have patience, stay prayed up, keep the faith, and seek God, we can learn what our purpose is. Trust the Lord. He will guide you.

Trust in the LORD WITH ALL THINE HEART; AND LEAN NOT UNTO THINE OWN UNDERSTANDING. IN ALL THY WAYS ACKNOWLEDGE HIM, AND HE SHALL DIRECT THY PATHS. (PROV. 3:5–6, KJV)

In moving forward, I remembered this scripture:

Faith is being sure of what we hope for, and certain of what we do not see. (Heb. 11:1)

In February 2015, I experienced a *spiritual interaction*. I heard a voice, saying, "Write a story about your pastor." It didn't just pass by, nor just go through my mind and was then gone. No! No! When the spiritual interaction came back a second time, that sent up a red flag. It encouraged me to wonder what it was all about and why I was receiving it. I don't write!

Even though I was confused, did not have an answer, and did not know what it all meant, I still felt I needed to do something, but I didn't really know what to do. At a time like that, I believe most people would probably remove it from their minds so they can move on with their lives and pretend nothing had happened.

But now I wonder, why did I think I had to be different and figure out what was going on? It had to be the Holy Spirit, not me! As I have stated already, God will select you to fulfill an assignment for Him. We are His children, and faith begins with belief. We should try to understand, because living by faith also requires that we put our souls under the control of our Spirit. When we have a personal relationship with God, He will give us visions, and He will use our hands, feet, and eyes to fulfill an assignment. Trust in Him.

When it came back to me the third time, like *out of nowhere*, that really got my attention. So to keep from feeling like I was going crazy, I decided to try and find out what the purpose was . . . and why me? Also, I felt that I was dealing with the unknown, and I was wondering if it was real. I did not have a clear mind and didn't know which way to turn.

After the voice had come into my mind *three times, saying the same thing,* I figured there had to be a reason. I was puzzled, did not have a clear mind-set, and needed an answer. Without realizing what I was doing, I said, "Why me . . . why me?" And I just walked off and tried not to think about it.

After a few days, there was a voice that said, "Because you know him!"

I thought to myself, *Know him? No, I do not!* Because my pastor is the most private person I have ever met. So *I do not know him!*

After making that statement, I said to myself, "What are you doing?" I did not have an answer. I thought about Jesus and the things He did. Also, my parents came to my mind and reminded me that if you walk with the Lord, He will guide you.

After standing there in silence for a moment, thinking about the words *You know him. You know him!* it all came to me. I realized that I had been chosen and given an assignment from the Lord. *I believe it was led by the Holy Spirit.*

I said, "Lord, I got it now! You want the people to know about your servant and you want me to tell his story to the world." No, I don't know him. But I do know about him.

I said, "Lord, for twenty-eight years, I have served as his administrative assistant. And, yes, I have learned some things about his servant work. I know about his commitment to You, Lord, and Your people. I know about his character, his caring spirit, his preaching and teaching of the holy Word. Lord, if that is what You are asking me to do, I accept the assignment! And with Your help, I will do all I can to write the *story* about his servanthood, faith, belief, and accomplishments. I am willing to move this vision to reality. And, Lord, I am truly honored and thankful that You sent me to this church to groom me for such a time as this. It was Your plan and my purpose. What a mighty God You are. To You, Lord, I give the glory!"

According to the scriptures, I do believe that God will give us assignments to fulfill His plans, as He has just done for me. Also, we are taught that He gives each of His children a destiny before we are born. If we stay on *the Christian journey, be faithful, and trust in Him, we will be able to reach our destiny!*

Welcome home, my good and faithful servant.

I did not accept this opportunity to fulfill the assignment because I thought it would be easy. No! That was not the case. I had never written a story about anyone. I had never printed nor published a book. So I accepted it because I knew I had a *great servant* to write about and I knew I had the *greatest story writer* in the world by my side. But, most of all, it was an assignment that God had given to me. I knew He would equip me to do the job, and He would never leave me alone.

God gives us assignments every day. Some of us fulfill them and some of us do not realize that God is asking us to be His hands, eyes, and body here on earth. Try to think of a time that you felt the presence of God but were not really listening to Him and truly had no desire to attempt to say, "Yes, Lord! Please direct me, let me know what You want me to do and I will strive to do it."

This message is to let you know that it isn't too late to start listening to God! He has a plan for you and want you to fulfill the purpose He has for you, release your potential, and accept His assignment. What's for you *is* for you. If you don't fulfill it, you will take it to the grave with you. Trust God and never say no to Him!

Understanding the Threefold Purpose

That assignment was very challenging, and it had a threefold purpose. One was to tell about a "faithful pastor with a heart to serve." Another was, "to bestow honor to him for his fifty years of service" at the same church, St. Paul MBC. Then, "to emphasize the legacy that was bestowed upon him from his father," and now he has passed it on down to his two sons who are in the ministry. That alone was *a story worth telling*.

Another challenge I thought I would have was to be able to get all the information I needed to present his true life story. But when I asked the Lord to help me because I did not know what to do, He stepped in and gave me everything I needed. After all, it was His story and He knew what He wanted the people to know. So, it was not going to be a hard assignment. In a unique way, it provided me the opportunity to uncap my talents and tap my hidden potentials and become a writer and an author. *Won't God do it?*

Also, it was in my thoughts to insert encouraging messages in the hopes that all who read the story would be blessed by the story and book. The imaginative style *that I decided to use* displayed a key role for the expressions that would be shown by a great group of committed servants through their expressions. See how they displayed determination, perseverance, faith, and hope. They believed *in God*, so they kept *trying* until they achieved their goal.

The road you travel might be hard. No matter what, keep traveling, because each of us comes into the world with an assignment to fulfill. If we don't accept and fulfill our responsibilities, the next generation may be lost also.

What God gives to you is for you. *Do not give up!* A quitter never wins; a winner never quits. You might have to forget your yesterday; just learn from your mistakes and press forward, no looking back, because God is trying to use you. Always strive to reach your goal. It truly enhances the knowledge, *for true service, just take the next step*—activate, stimulate, and ask God to guide you. *Glorify God!*

We must remember that God is always with us in everything. Ask the Lord for guidance, direction, wisdom, and understanding. He will give it to you.

The way my vision came to me, I thought it was to write a play. So I kept writing. I visualized a stage with students acting the parts of the story, which was exciting. Therefore, I decided to contact a few students and friends of the servant I was writing about. I thought that would be great to have family, friends, and members in this play. I wanted to see if they were interested in being in a play. I was not able to get young adults in the church due to their schedules.

I contacted two colleges to see if I could use their chapels to present a play. The request was exciting to them and they were willing to assist me. I still was not able to get actors. So those efforts were not successful. With a play still in my mind, I went to a high school in the neighborhood to seek assistance through their drama classes. This was in the hope that they would use this story to create a play and those students could present the play. After the visit there, I was never contacted. That was a disappointment.

So I continued to write; I researched addresses and sent letters and emails to Mr. Tyler Perry and Mr. Steve Harvey. I even called the TV stations, trying to get contact information for both, with no results. I contacted drama companies in Atlanta, seeking information on what to do to present a play and how to get actors. I was not successful with any of my efforts. I never gave up. I kept my faith and hope alive. I stayed on the journey so I could fulfill the promise I made to the Lord. I knew He was still with me, because I was still so happy and excited with the accomplishment I had made with the writing of the story.

My determination and desire to follow the vision kept me striving to fulfill the dream. As I got closer to completing the story, I realized I had to come up with a plan. I went to the pastor and told him that I was going to write a story about his life to reflect his servanthood. (He did not know that I was already writing the story—nor did anyone else know.) After a few moments of silence, he looked up and said, "Okay, if that's what you want to do." I said thanks and left.

I will admit that I was confused and did not really know why things were not going as I wanted them to. Later, I remembered that it was a vision given to me by the Lord. In His time, He would let me know what to do. Even with that thought, I had a concern and really wanted to make sure I was doing what the Lord wanted me to do. I wanted to refocus and reconnect with God. That was the only way I would be able to move forward. Even though He gave me the vision, it was still in His hands, and I must follow His directions. Not following His lead would not get me where I needed to go. We must have patience, always wait; let God work through us, show Him that we are serving Him, and know He is in control of everything. Be thankful and give Him praises.

I continued with the writing, but I was not really pleased because I was not moving forward with the play. I was wondering why it was not working out. I kept praying to the Lord and asking Him, "Lord, why is this not working, nor moving forward? Why did I not get a call from the school, and why have I not been able to get any actors? Lord, please tell me what you want me to do so I can move forward."

I ended my prayer and exercised patience. I knew there had to be a reason and only He had the answer. So all I could do was keep the faith and believe in God. I just kept moving on with my life.

We should never try to jump ahead of God nor try to rush Him. Just know He will never leave us and He will continue to direct us. So let's be willing to wait on Him.

After a few days, my questions were answered. While sitting in the room, it came into my mind. Out of the clear, blue sky, I heard these words. "You need a story first in order to have a play."

I sat there, thinking, *What does that mean? I am writing a play and now I am hearing that I need a story.* Then it came to me. So that is the reason I have not been moving forward—that's not His plan. I said, "Lord, where did I go wrong? Please show me the way, so I can regain my focus."

Yes, there are times when we get our focuses mixed up. Therefore, we should not try to move forward with anything unless we go to Him for guidance. And it could not be that we feel we don't need God to guide us; it could be that we are so happy about what we are doing that we forget that it is by His will that we will move forward. I then knew what I needed to do to move to the next level, and that was for me to step back and wait on Him. I thought, *How did I get ahead of myself and thought I could move forward without Him?*

So, as you see, He stepped in and got me focused as He showed me how to move things forward. That was a lesson I learned very fast. Then I realized why it was not moving forward. I had a silent moment with Him and said, "Lord, I am so sorry. Please forgive me and please tell me what you want me to do. Because I feel that you have left me at a fork in the road, and I really don't know which turn to take. Please help me."

I knew I had to seek the Lord and ask for guidance. After a few days, it came to my mind to just start changing the format of the writing and focused on a story without having to start over. As a matter of fact, it was a blessing that I had so much in place already; it was easy to refocus. I just kept thanking the Lord, praying, listening, and writing.

As I moved from the fork in the road, I felt that I was on the road that the Lord wanted me to be traveling. I continued writing and everything was moving forward. In a few months, I had completed a draft of the story. I was really amazed with the progress I had already made. I was so excited and wanted to let the pastor know that I had really written a story to reflect his life. But I knew I would wait on the Lord to show me when and how to do that. My patience came back to me and I just waited because I knew it would be in His time. I kept reading the story to make sure it was interesting, correct, and complete. But most of all, I wanted it to be an inspiring story that everyone who reads it would like it and tell others.

During one of the Wednesday night services, it came into my mind to ask the pastor if I could meet with him for a few moments. He said yes. I went into his office, during the change of the class. He was sitting at his desk when I entered the room. He looked up.

I said, "Pastor, I have written a story about your life."

He just sat and looked at me for a few moments. Then he asked, "Have you published it?"

I said, "No, sir. I would not do that without your permission."

A smile came on his face. "Will I get to see it before you print it?"

"Yes, sir." Then I pulled my hand from behind my back and handed him a draft of the story. I said, "Sir, please read it and let me know what you think or what changes you may have." Then I left his office.

Well, months passed by and he never said a word about the story. I did not say anything to him either. Other things were going on in the church, and as always, I was busy. I did not work on the story; I put that behind me. But I really wanted to know if I had fulfilled my promise to the Lord to write the story. Also, I was praying that the pastor would like the story, be pleased, and approve his life story that I had written. Yes, all that was on my mind. When you are given an assignment, it's natural for you to hope that you have done a great job. You want everything to be in order, and you really want the story to be correct.

Most of all, it is important that the pastor accept the story about his life and legacy that I have written. I needed to know that I had fulfilled that assignment. I decided to just wait and see.

One day, the pastor asked me to come to his office for a moment. Once I got in the office, he said, "I know you gave me this a while back. But I did not read it right away. I did not know what you had written about me."

Well, that was not an unusual thought when you are writing about someone's life. So, I just stood there. After all, I have worked for him and with him for many years. But we all know that a story can take any turn, and I did not know how he felt about it. So I just stood there.

After a few moments, he said, "I do like the story, and you can move forward with it. But I would like to see it after it is finished and before you publish it."

I assured him that I would not move forward before letting him see it. I reminded him that I was working on his fiftieth pastoral anniversary and his banquet, so I will have to wait until that ended. He was pleased and I was happy and excited. I asked him not to tell anyone about it. I had not worked on the book for months, but knew I would return to it. Deep in my heart, I believed that God had given me this vision and I wanted to be obedient to Him.

Also, I saw this as an opportunity to use my talents and tell the world about this steadfast servant of the Lord. One who has been on the battlefield for fifty years, at the same church, serving the people of God. In addition, maybe I felt that it was a story worth writing and I felt honored that God had given me a vision to tell the world about a committed servant, one who has devoted his life to teaching and preaching His Word to the people. One who was following Jesus's plan when He told His disciples, "Go ye into all the world and preach the gospel to every creature." I was so pleased with the assignment.

When I decided to start writing again, I was not sure in which direction to go, since I had not been successful in getting people to accept being in the play. In my prayers, I asked the Lord to guide and direct my thoughts. I wanted to move forward but felt that I was at a standstill. I reminded the Lord that it was His vision and I needed His help. A few days later, it came into my spirit that I needed a story before performing a play. I thought about it for a few days and was really confused. So I just waited.

I had the opportunity to go on a mini vacation with my husband. The peace and contentment were truly what I needed. Time away made a difference. My mind was refreshed, and I was able to focus. I started writing again, but in a different direction. I was no longer focused on a play. Instead,

I just continued writing the story. To move forward, I decided to go to a website to research how to publish a book, since my efforts for the play were not working out. I contacted a couple of publishing companies to discover how to move forward. I got a lot of information; I was ready and encouraged. After researching and talking with the agency, I decided that I would utilize the service of a publishing company, and get the book published.

I started having health challenges and ended up in the hospital for a few days. After that, I decided to rest awhile before moving forward with the book. A few months passed and then I became excited about completing the book. I felt that when you are willing to move forward with faith, you must know and trust God. Not just know of Him but be willing to believe in His love and promises, because that is all you need. That alone will take you to the end of the journey. That is how I felt after I stopped wondering how to move the vision to reality. I wanted to be victorious, obedient, and to fulfill the vision by telling the story of this great servant. I stayed on course and decided I would do whatever was necessary to complete the mission, so there would be a story that reflected the servanthood of a great man.

Just as I was finishing the book, I got a call one day from a person who had been in my life many years ago. I did not really remember her, but I did not tell her. It was strange to me that she came back into my life. Especially since I didn't really remember who she was, and we had not been talking. I knew she knew me, because she said, "How is Ted doing?"

Now, that was a shock. I thought, *She knows us?* So, we would talk from time to time. One day, we were talking, and her phone went dead. I looked at the number and called her. It went to voicemail that said, "Leave a message for April Wooden."

I said to myself, "I don't remember April Wooden." I could not place her as someone I truly knew.

When my husband got home, I asked him if he knew April Wooden.

He said, "No. Who is that?"

I said, "I don't really know. She called the other day and told me she was back in Atlanta and asked me how you were doing." He looked at me *in a funny way* and kept walking.

Well, after a few phone conversations, April asked, "What are you doing now in your life?" That was a strange thing to hear and I felt strange about it and didn't know why.

After thinking for a moment, out of nowhere, I heard myself say, "You would not believe it, but I am writing a book."

The question came back, "What kind of book?"

After talking about the book a few times, she said, "I can help you with it, if you are ready to publish it."

I did not know what to say. But in my mind, I was thinking, *How will she be able to help me publish a book, why did she show up at this time, or am I dreaming?* That was another crossroad and I didn't know what to do or say. Put yourself in my place. I was standing there trying to figure out how all of this came together and where was it coming from? And then I thought, it has to be, from the Lord. This is what came to my mind: *Where is this coming from?* Writing that story was between the Lord and me. I never really told anyone that I was writing a story, nor did I go to others about what I should do or how I should do it—the Spirit had shown me what I needed. And I stayed on the straight and narrow road, which kept my focus on God, for directions and not on my directions for this assignment.

At this point, I did not know what to do. However, I did believe that when God was ready for me to seek advice, He would send someone that He had equipped for this purpose. Since I had been writing for a year and now I was coming close to the ending of the story, He sent April Wooden. Someone I had not talked to for years, and now He sent her back into my life at a time such as this. But it was still strange to me, because we were not really friends. I knew of her, because I would see her when I went to get my car serviced and we would talk a little. When she got married, she invited us to the wedding. We went, but after that, I did not see her again. I was told that she and her husband moved to another state. I supposed meeting her, way back then, was His plan, years before I was inspired by a vision to write a story about my pastor.

God Is Amazing

He made plans for me even though I didn't know why I had met her years in advance. See how God worked in my life after I accepted the assignment? He used her to help me move forward with the vision. He already had a plan and a purpose for me, years before it was revealed to me. And He had a plan for her also. That is how He work in our lives. So we need to always stay focused on Him.

As believers, we must trust, pray, and ask God to direct us. There are times when we don't know what to do and how to move forward with what we are trying to do. When we study His words, it will direct us. He said, "I am with you always, seek me and I will be found." Meaning, He will not put us out there and leave us. So when it seems that things are going wrong, or you don't know what to do after you have tried your best to accomplish a mission, that is when you should go back to Him.

He said, "Knock and the door will be open to you." Just go to the Lord, and ask Him to direct you in the direction He wants you to go. Believe and have faith that He will direct you.

We should never think that we don't need Him. Our success comes through Him. Give it a try and you will see. We must stay focused on Him and see the work, He will do through you that others will see His work and praise Him. We must believe that, because He knows what is best for us and the direction He wants us to go. What a faithful God we have. When we think about it, we will see how God has already prepared everything, and we never think about it. People come into our lives for a purpose . . . that is because it is God's plan. We must stop trying to get ahead of God's plan to make it our plan. Instead, keep the faith, pray, and believe in Him. He will give you wisdom, knowledge, and understanding when we believe in Him. It came to my spirit to move from the crossroad. There are no answers there for me.

I had to decide if I wanted to pursue this or step back. After I thought about it, I decided to invite her to church, and I could talk with her more. April accepted the invitation. I told Ted about April and that she has accepted to go to church with us. He said, "Do you really remember her and when you really met her?"

I said, "I am not sure, but I think I know her. So, can we pick her up from the train station?"

He said, "How can you pick up someone you don't really know?"

I said, "I understand, but I really want to meet her." In my mind, I said, "God got it!"

On the way to meet her, I did not know if I was going to remember her or not. But for some unknown reason, I felt I had to go on with it and see what the end would bring. When I got to the train station to pick her up, I was not sure what I was going to do if I did not remember her. But as we sat there, I prayed and felt that God would work it out. So I was at peace with it, and I believed that the Lord was directing me, and it was going to be okay.

So we sat and waited. I received a call and April said, "I am coming out now, I have on a blue blouse."

A feeling of release came upon me. I said, "Thank you, Lord." I told her where we were sitting in the truck. When we saw a lady with a blue blouse come out, I did not know she would be a white lady. I was really confused and did not know if she was the right person. I did not know if I should call out her name or wait to see if she was going to come toward us. After all, I did tell her what we were driving. I sat there, trying to recall if I knew this person. When April saw the truck, she came our way.

Ted went into action. He got out of the truck and went over to meet her. *He saw that I was not able to move.* Ted said,

"How are you doing? I know it has been a long time, so when and where did we meet you?"

She said, "I met you all when you came to buy your Volvo cars. And you all came to our wedding."

At that moment, the light bulb went on in my head and some of the memories came back, especially the car dealer, then the wedding on the lawn. I did not see her after that, and we never did anything together other than talking when I went to the dealer. Yes, it still was strange to me, for her to still remember me and my phone number. That had to be a reason. However, no memories came back to Ted. But he played it off well as we drove to church.

It was a great reunion and church was wonderful. We went to eat and took her back to the station. After a couple of meetings and a lot of talking, it was like a dream came back to me. Also, I realized that it was another blessing that had come back into my life at this time. I also discovered that it was going to enhance what I was trying to do with my book. After all, I did not know what and how to move the book forward. April went out of her way to assist me with moving forward and the opportunity to fulfill the dream with one of her friends. Later, I discovered that her friend was Dr. Evan Money. I checked him out on the web and right off, I knew another blessing had come from the Lord. He was still leading, guiding, and equipping me. I never thought this would happen. Now, I realize, that it was God's plan, many,

many years ago, because that is how He is. He had put all of this in place before he gave me the assignment. They both came into my life just when I needed help. Only God would plan like that. I felt safe, even though I did not really know either one of them.

They explained everything to me and gave documents to confirm what they were saying. But at times, I thought, *Maybe this is just a set up.* I would go into prayer and ask the Lord for guidance. I always felt refreshed and peaceful after talking with the Lord. I trusted April and Evan. After receiving a contract, invoice, and other details, I felt safe with her decision to trust them and let them lead me to the victory they kept talking about. After reviewing Dr. Evan's website, I was satisfied, overwhelmed, and excited. I knew God was in the plan. So everything was put in place.

The one thing I thought a lot about was when Dr. Money called and asked me to email him my book document. Yes, I admit that I thought for a moment. Knowing that I didn't have a copyright on the document, *and I am sending it to him.* But I felt good and I trusted the Lord. It all went just fine. After he reviewed the book, he called and told me how he would handle everything. None of it made any sense to me. I knew nothing about doing something like this. I am glad the Lord knew that, and He took over. When you truly put your trust in Him, things will happen. I was truly impressed with the service Dr. Money was providing.

I suppose the statement he made when he called remained with me. He said, "This is a great story and I am so pleased that you were obedient to the Lord, for writing this book. I will give you a discount, since you are a friend of April. Also, I will have your book proofed, edited, I will put it on Amazon, and I will get it registered in the Library of Congress, in Washington, DC."

There was joy, all around me. *Who wouldn't serve a God like this?* All the transaction was taken care of and everything went into actions. Oh, what a relief it was. I was so thankful to the Lord.

During the early planning for the publishing of the book, I would meet with April Wooden at the well-known Kupcakerie.

We would review documents and make decisions on how to move forward. April, being a friend, was really an inspiration in my life at that time. The mother and her son were so nice and they supported me.

Everything was going great and I was so happy. The end of the year was coming up. I wanted the book ready before January. I got a call one day and was told that the book had been proofed, edited, and was ready for printing, but I needed to design the cover and send the information I wanted on the back and front of the cover. I was truly lost. *Cover, cover,* I kept saying to myself. I asked them what I should put on the back cover. They said, "Whatever you think, would encourage them to buy the book, a picture of you, and a brief bio."

I sat for a moment. I said, "Lord, I need you to help me with the cover. I went on the website, to get a suggestion. I found an image that I thought would be okay for the cover and added the title.

I sat down and asked the Lord to give me what I should put on the back cover. After a while, visions started coming to me, and I starting writing. An hour later, I called them and told them I was sending them the information. I got a call back and the guy asked, "Is that what you really want on the front cover?"

I did not know what to say. He said, "I will help you out. Tell me a little about the person you are writing about, and I will design something for you." What a relief that was. The next day, he sent a copy of what I sent him and a copy of what he designed, and said, "Let me know which one you want." Oh, my goodness. The design he created was awesome.

I sent these words, "For the one I sent . . . delete, delete!" He had designed such a beautiful cover. I was so happy. I will never show what I had sent him. A few days later, I received a package with a copy of the book cover. I was so proud and could not stop thanking the Lord. I reviewed it and gave them permission to print it.

I talked with the pastor and asked him if I could let the congregation know that I had written a book about your servanthood. He said, "Yes, and we decided the date." I could not get a finished copy by December. The Library of Congress had not listed the book, so I told him that was fine. I asked them to send me the final draft of the cover, and I would enlarge it. That went over very well. I made plans to make a special announcement to the church members on December 18, 2016. The thought of doing that was very rewarding to me. I wanted them to know about the assignment the Lord had given to me and how He had blessed me to complete the task.

When I made my special announcement that I had written a book to reflect the life and the legacy of our pastor, Rev. Clayton E. Taylor Sr., D., Min., I could see that they were really surprised. They didn't know I was surprised also. I never thought I would be an author. Only God knew it. Because it was His plan. I felt good when some of the members gave praises to me, as a rising author, at St. Paul M.B.C.

A Celebration Time for Me

1

I was giving praises to the Lord for that *milestone*. It inspired me to keep on trusting and believing in God. I was filled with joy that I had accepted the vision from the Lord and made it a reality by being obedient and surrendering to His will to fulfill His purpose. That experience will be in my mind forever. During the celebration, the Youth Voices in Praise Choir stood around the sanctuary and sung a song that I changed around.

+We Just Love Our Pastor+

(In the tune of "Jesus Loves Me")

Chorus:

Yes, we just love him, yes, we just love him; yes, we just him, we thank our God for him. Pastor is our Preacher Man, he teaches us what he can

He directs us in our lives, so we can see our Christ.

He is here to guide us home; we are happy and not alone.

We do listen to his word, and he know what we have heard.

We thank Pastor for his work, we thank him for Your love.

We are blessed to have him here; we raise our hands in cheer.

Yes, we just love Him . . . He is our pastor.

I gave the Pastor a certificate and a copy of the book cover. Pastor Taylor was truly appreciative that I had written a story to reflect his servanthood on his Christian journey for fifty plus years . . . preaching, teaching, and *serving the people of God*!

From vision to reality.

There is a promise and a reward

when we serve God.

We should never miss our blessings.

Just say yes and receive your reward.

He will guide you.

Book Celebration

New Year's Day celebration at the home of my neice, Mary Salter-Clausell in recognition of my book

Everlean Merritt (Williams)

(from left to right - Everlean - Mary)

Husband, nieces, nephew, sister, cousin, and friends attended this second celebration in honor of the author.

Book Celebration
Alabama . . . Alabama

After talking with my sister, Estelle Roster, I talked with a library staff member. I asked if I could schedule a book signing in February, during Black History Month. The request was granted. This was great for me to go back home for a celebration—*as a rising author*. I attended and graduated from BIA, later named Union High.

I was so excited and so thankful for the opportunity to display my book in the library for others to see, read, and purchase. Most of all, I was very appreciative and happy to return to my hometown and let others know the blessings from the Lord, to encourage them that He would do the same for them if they strive for a personal relationship with Him and ask Him to reveal the purpose He has for them so they can experience Him. He is waiting on them. To God I give the *glory*!

Alabama Book Celebration Words of Appreciation

To Mrs. Mary Harris, *an angel in the right place, at the right time.* I thank *you* for your encouraging words, spirit of caring, service, and commitment, which was displayed in your character during the preparation for the book signing celebration in my honor.

Many thanks to the newspaper in my hometown, Monroeville, Alabama, for the nice article to help spread the good news in that town where I was accepted to be at the library for a book signing. I am honored that the Lord chose me for the assignment and thankful for the insight from the Holy Spirit in writing the story. Now, I am truly pleased that I was able to complete a story that became a book to reflect the life of my pastor, Rev. Clayton E. Taylor Sr., D. Min.

This experience will be with me the rest of my life. I learned that we all may have dreams. But to make dreams come into reality, it takes a lot of faith, prayer, belief, determination, dedication, self-discipline, effort, guidance, commitment, other people, and God, who will bring you through.

He did it for me and He will do it for you. Just put your trust in Him and experience His work for you. You, too, can make your vision become a reality.

Success is to be measured not so much by the position that one has reached in life as by the obstacles which he has overcome while trying to succeed. (Booker T. Washington)

I express my thanks for your assistance in making the Black History event a grand celebration for me and everyone who attended.

Many thanks to the staff of the Monroe County Library, in Monroeville, Alabama, for hosting my book signing event, Saturday, February 25, 2017.

CONGRATULATIONS FOR EVERLEAN MERRITT

Monroe County Library has been in the formal LaSalle Hotel building since 1984. It is listed on the Alabama Register of Landmarks/Heritage and is included in the Monroeville Downtown Historic District listed on the National Register of Historic Places.

During the preparation for the movie *To Kill a Mockingbird*, Gregory Peck visited Monroeville, Alabama. As young students, we were excited when we heard the movie would be performed in our hometown and we were waiting to see it. During one of his visits, we were able to see him. I have visited the courthouse many times where the movie was held. I took the Golden Pioneers, from our church, St. Paul MBC, in East Point, Georgia to Monroeville, to visit the *To Kill a Mockingbird* library. They enjoyed it.

Classmates, friends, and family came to the library to fellowship . . . and to buy a book!

Your life is what you make it

A Thought for Going Back Home

Your journey should be interesting to those who know you and have spent time with you. I will admit that I thought about how it would be to see the people whom I knew when I lived there, ones I went to school with and graduated with. I left and didn't really keep in touch with everyone. I didn't know if they would be glad to see me, congratulate me, and support me for success. I didn't dwell on that; I prayed and left it in God's hand. The following words came to me, *Never burn your bridges, because you might want to cross over them again.* A smile came on my face, because I knew I had not mistreated anyone and I moved on.

I am proud to say that I truly enjoyed my visit when I went back to my hometown for my book signing. It was great to see everyone, smiling, hugging, and saying, "How are you doing?" The fun and fellowship time were great and brought refreshing memories of the good times of togetherness, love, and renewing of friendship from the old days. Most of all, I truly appreciated them for buying a copy of my book. I have been in touch with some of them since that visit and think of them often. It came to me to put the pictures of the celebrations so we will always have those memories, even though we might not see each other often. I know I will remember them.

Friendship Is a Blessing from God

When you show love, live according to His word, others will see Him through your spiritual walk and your service. Stay focused and trust the Lord.

Book Celebration for the Author
MARCH 8, 2017

Celebration and a luncheon were hosted by cousins.

Celebration and Book Signing For a Rising Author at St. Paul Missionary Baptist Church, East Point, Georgia

The writing of a story to reflect the life of a faithful servant.

By: Everlean Merritt-Williams

The story highlights the importance of serving and God's reward. Serving enables you to grow in Christian maturity. It enhances your knowledge and help you comprehend. It clarifies the principles of God's Word. It encourages commitment, faith, and confidence.

Rev. Dr. Clayton E. Taylor Sr.

Is Highlighted in This Story

*Book Title: *Do You Know the Man*

+Join in The Book-Signing.

Celebration and Congratulations

My wonderful pastor, Rev. Clayton E.Taylor SR., D. MIN.
"A Faithful Pastor with a Heart to Serve."

A servant that has given fifty-three plus years preaching and teaching the word of God. He reminds us that to receive the promises of God, we must obey the principles of God. Our devoted and caring first lady, Mrs. Christine Taylor, has a heart of love and a smile that shines like a star! We love both of them for their caring spirit and service to others.

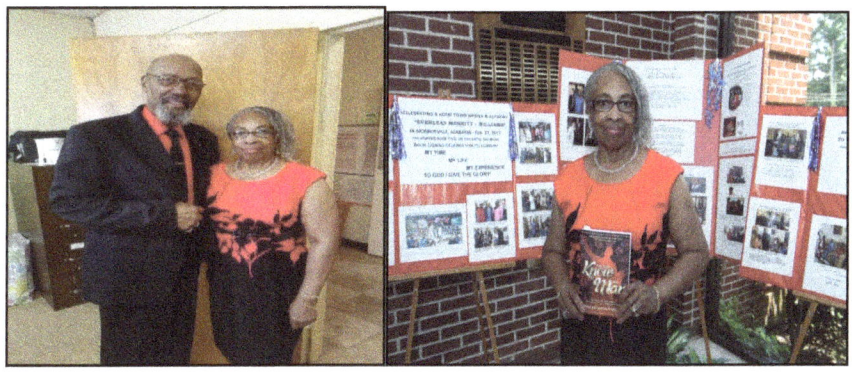

My beloved husband, SFC Theodore (Ted) Merritt. He is the other rock in my life! He meets no stranger; he will go out of his way to help anyone and always has an encouraging word to share. Our life together has been wonderful and I am glad God sent him into my life. We still celebrate our Friday's date . . . days or nights.

Family at the Book Signing

Church members at the book signing.

Friends who came for the book signing.

Remarks from the Author

Surrender to the Lord

He obscures you; He watches you; He knows your heart, and He knows everything about you. He expects us to show love, trust, and have faith for a rewarding life. But, most of all, we must know who we believe and who will always be there for us. When we really think about our life's journey, there must be a moment when we think and wonder, Do I know why I am here and what is my purpose?

To know the answer, we must go to the person, *Jesus the Christ,* who created us. Ask Him to give you wisdom, knowledge, and understanding. In His giving and in His time, He will reveal your purpose. Be thankful, obedient, and willing to serve. Watch how He will work in you. What an experience that would be. I am so happy, thankful, and blessed, that He thought enough of me to give me an assignment and equipped me to accomplish my goal. To Him, I give the glory! I could not have done it without Him! He expresses His love in so many ways; we just need to be ready when He invites us to serve and lift Him up, so others will see the work He is doing through us. Because without Him, we can't do anything. Also, when we accept His invitation, He will put other people in your life to help you in your serving. God wants unity and togetherness, so love and appreciation can be expressed when you are serving and others will see your commitment for what you are doing as pleasing Him! *Always praise God.*

I am happy to say that I experienced that when I said to the Holy Spirit, "Lord, I will accept your invitation, without regret, no matter what happens. I will write a story about my pastor to reflect his servanthood and his legacy, with Your help."

That is the best decision I had made. What a joy it was to have a personal relationship with God, to experience Him and fulfill His will for my life. It brought so much happiness and peace to my heart and my soul as tears ran down my face and excitement glowing through my mind, as I was giving praises to the Lord for the assignment. At that moment, I thought about my parents and started thanking God for giving me great parents who taught me about the love and the goodness of the Lord. Even though I knew they were in heaven, I felt that they were looking down on me. How blessed I was and how thankful I am.

"Understanding God's predestined plan for your life is a powerful tool for maturing you in the Faith."

Encouragement for Growth

Always remember, Jesus was not just a point in time, but the focal point of all time; not just a life, but the wellspring of life itself. The three years of his ministry, culminating in His death and resurrection, formed the heart and soul of our faith. So, If God is I Am, then who am I? Jesus is the password to a better life. Share His love with someone every day. That will keep you encouraged. God is the way; focus on Him for direction, He will never fail, nor leave you. To move forward, we must stay connected to God. We must have staying power. When you connect with God through *Jesus the Christ*, it will enable the weak, those who don't know what to do, or think they can't fulfill a mission … they only have to trust Him and remain strong! So, when we pray, we must make sure that we are praying from the heart. Because we may just be praying ourselves out of a lifetime. That may be the reason *so many of us* tend to become seasons in another person's life. Please don't follow others, only follow the Lord.

Let Go and Let God Believe and Walk in Faith

I hope this story will encourage you.

On my journey, I have truly been blessed. I have achieved goals, completed assignments, received many certificates, I have had very good jobs, and I've traveled to many places.

I will say, all that brought joy and happiness to my life. It provided proof that if you believe, it can bring you blessings from the Lord... all things are possible, *if it is His will for your life*. But let me remind you! It did not come easy. I was blessed because of my prayers, patience, faith, belief, determination, obedience, commitment, perseverance, and for *trust in Jesus, the Christ. Just a*ccept His invitation when the Spirit brings it to you.

Words of Appreciation

Thanks to everyone. My wonderful family who supported me with my first book. Those who purchased a book, and the ones who expressed their congratulations to me. Many thanks to the members of my church, Jackie Westry and James Ellis, for their support. The staff at the Atlanta Braves; the members of the Fifth District–GMBC; people from various churches; friends in Texas, Alabama, Nashville, Florida; ex-coworkers from East Point Police; and those who purchased a book from Amazon. I cannot list all their names . . . but I say thanks. You made a difference in my life, as I experienced God and the Holy Spirit that brought me through . . . *with His grace and mercy*!

To my pastor, I thank you for believing in me and giving me the opportunity to share your life story and legacy with the world! I believe that many people know about You, but don't really know You. We, your church family, are truly blessed to have you, as our leader, teacher, and pastor. Your messages and sermons always give a clear picture of the scripture, with understanding of His Word that are truly from the Bible. It gives hope for the week and provides knowledge to those who are striving for Christian maturity. We are blessed and glad to have you as our pastor, we thank God!

Picture of the Taylor's family in Georgia.

Author's Profile

Everlean Merritt-Williams

Everlean is a happy and caring person. Her early life was lived on a large farm, with her family, which was very rewarding to her. She learned a lot, from her parents. Her father, the late Fletcher Williams Sr., and her mother, the late Marcella Woods Williams. She is so glad she was raised in a Christian home with ten siblings. Her father and mother taught their eleven children about Jesus Christ and right from wrong. They told them, "You can do anything you want to do, and always think for yourself."

Her spiritual journey started at an early age. She enjoyed singing in the choir and VBS. Even though Everlean's life started in Alabama, where she attended and completed high school, it did not stop there. Her new life's journey took her throughout the United State and to the Bahamas. She spent time in New York, and Nashville, Tennessee. There, she married her first husband, the late Leonard Bell. They had a happy life together with their daughter.

After the early death of her first husband, they moved to St. Louis for a year and moved back to Nashville. She decided to continue her education. She entered college and graduated with honors from Tennessee State University, Nashville, Tennessee. There, she met and married SFC Theodore Merritt, and they have enjoyed thirty-nine happy years of marriage. It provided her the opportunity to accompany him to Europe. They visited thirteen countries during those three years. She experienced a military style of living with their blended family, three girls, now six grandchildren, and one great-granddaughter.

Her professional work life started at Fisk University in Nashville, Tennessee. Then, Tennessee State Government, The Tennessee General Assembly Treasurer's Department. Then, Tennessee State University, Public Relations. In Germany, she operated and managed the Learning Resource Center, US Army, Germany. She taught one year for the University of Maryland, in Germany.

Her husband was transferred to Texas. She worked with the Texas Human Resource Department. She moved to Atlanta when her husband retired from the military. From 1989 until her retirement in 2005, she worked with the City of East Point and the Police Department. Also, she managed a grant for the Department of Defense for the Weed and Seed initiative. After retirement, she worked in the Clayton County School System for six years.

In 1988, Everlean united with the St. Paul Missionary Baptist Church, when her husband reunited with his church family. After she joined, she served with various ministries, organized a youth ministry, a women's ministry, and she coordinated special events. Her commitment and devoted spirit were noticed by many, including her pastor. In 1996, Pastor Taylor asked her to serve as his administrative assistant. She accepted and is still serving in that position. Also, she served and assisted the ministries with special events.

Everlean's and her husband's beautiful relationship and marriage, which have a true foundation with the Lord, is observed by many. They still enjoy traveling, they continue to honor their "date day/night" commitment, to devote Fridays spending time with each other.

This devoted worker, who has accomplished a lot in life, is off to another life's journey. Out of nowhere, she was inspired by a vision to write a story that expressed the service of her pastor, who has devoted fifty-three years serving at the same church, striving to tell everybody about somebody who could save anybody. That experience made a difference in her life. The vision was fulfilled and books were purchased. She learned so much during that time, and now, she has decided to continue writing. Her desire is to encourage others to seek God *if you are interested in writing.* "He did it for me and He will do it for you. Let Him use you."

> +MOTTO+

Your life is what you make it. Strive to make it what you want it to be. Because you are not the victim of circumstances, but the product of your own decisions. Make good decisions.

> Many Thanks to You for Your Support.
> My purpose for writing this story.

I just want to help others, accomplish their goal.

My encouraging words are to inspire you!

All things are possible with the help of the Lord. Seek and follow Him!

He has a purpose for your life.

If you are given a vision or an opportunity to experience God, *go to the Lord in prayer.* Establish a personal relationship with Him and know that the Holy Spirit is there to direct you. You must believe, have patience, and be obedient, so the Lord can use you in His work . . . trust Him!

To: _____

Date:_____

Signature:

_____

www.ingramcontent.com/pod-product-compliance
Lightning Source LLC
LaVergne TN
LVHW050137080526
838202LV00061B/6507